THE INGREDIENTS OF A
LEADER

THE INGREDIENTS OF A
LEADER

DAVID D. BRISCOE

Copyright © 2018 by David D. Briscoe.

Library of Congress Control Number: 2018903600
ISBN: Hardcover   978-1-9845-1703-6
            Softcover   978-1-9845-1702-9
            eBook   978-1-9845-1701-2

All rights reserved. No part of this book may be reproduced or transmitted in any form or by any means, electronic or mechanical, including photocopying, recording, or by any information storage and retrieval system, without permission in writing from the copyright owner.

Any people depicted in stock imagery provided by Getty Images are models, and such images are being used for illustrative purposes only.
Certain stock imagery © Getty Images.

Print information available on the last page.

Rev. date: 03/21/2018

To order additional copies of this book, contact:
Xlibris
1-888-795-4274
www.Xlibris.com
Orders@Xlibris.com
775463

CONTENTS

Acknowledgments vii
Dedication ix
    1) Identity Change 1
    2) Inception 6
    3) Deception 12
    4) Development.. 17
    5) Metamorphosis 22
    6) Unity 28
    7) Opportunity 34
    8) Servitude.. 39
    9) Failure... 43
   10) The Prize 47

ACKNOWLEDGMENTS

THERE ARE SEVERAL people who played an important role in helping this book see the light of day. First, I wish to thank my wife and partner in crime, Jasmine, for all her love and support. On countless nights, she provided helpful feedback throughout every chapter. Jasmine has built my confidence as not only an author but as a man. She believed in the mission of publishing this book when it was just an idea and always encouraged me to stay hopeful. Behind every successful man, there is a woman who is even greater. My passion and love for Jasmine cannot be fully expressed in words, but I will try my best to express them. I want to say I love you with all my heart and soul. Thank you for never giving up on me, our marriage, our family and even our ministry. I can truly look at you and say that I have seen first-hand the Lord's grace and love manifested through you. Blessed is one who truly finds the person whom their soul loves.

Lastly, I want to thank my mother personally. My mom was a woman who refused to let her children quit. Doctors told my mom she could never bear a child after my older brother, Daniel, was born, but she always listened to the promises of God. Throughout every aspect of my life, whether it was a season of pure joy, depression or in-between, she has been right there fighting by my side. All my childhood memories were filled with all the sweet things she has done for me. I respect my mom to the fullest because was honest with me no matter how difficult it was to say it. Weeks before I moved down to Florida to start a new life, my mom and I got into an argument. Abruptly leaving the house in anger, when I was in the wrong, my mother called and texted me, apologized and told me to come home. Walking back into the house, I heard her praying for me; she always refused to allow division to seep through the crevices of her home. I owe my life to my mom for not just raising two kids on her own but for handing down the most important story ever told in history: the Gospel. Thank you for giving me the number one tool to succeed in life, and I will always tell your story to future generations of a courageous woman who laid down her life for her family, and most importantly, the Gospel of Jesus Christ. Love you, Mom!

DEDICATION

I want to dedicate this book to my wife, Jasmine, Izzak and Naomi. Also, my dad and my mom, including Dorrell, Daniel, Deanna, and Jonah. This book is also dedicated to my extended family, friends, spiritual family and Mrs. Jane Keil Yoder. Thank you for your love and support over the years. Your prayers and encouragement have molded and shaped me into the man I am today. I am forever indebted to you all.

1

Identity Change

*Never forget what you are, for surely the
world will not. Make it your strength.
Then it can never be your weakness. Armor yourself
in it, and it will never be used to hurt you.*

—George R.R. Martin

■ ■ ■

WHAT IS IDENTITY? Or better yet, what does identity mean to you? Identity can mean and create all different types of things. Some might find their identity in Christ, others might find their identity in assurance of money, and others find might their identity built on the premises of former or current accomplishments. Throughout this book, I am not going to dull you with statistics and peer-reviewed articles on what leadership is. We are going back to the basics, the root of leadership and how it is contextualized in any aspect.

Ingredients for any meal have a tendency to be few in number, but they are the driving force behind a remarkable meal. This book is somewhat short and small, but just like ingredients, it can create an impactful leader who is seasoned to perfection. Ponder that question again: What does identity mean to you? You probably are wondering why I keep asking you that. Identity is important because it marks the soul of who you are and who you will become in the future. Identity manifests in the way we lead, supervise, make decisions, persuade, form relationships, and negotiate responsibilities each day.[1] But how is identity shaped, how is it manifested, and where does it come from? Personally, I love to think of identity in a variety of ways, but there is one that pops into my mind. Buckle up, because I am about to take you on a wild roller coaster through my thoughts and what identity means to me.

Identity. Hmmm. Have you ever gone to a dealership and bought a car or a motorcycle? Or better yet, have you bought a car from a private dealer or a third-party website? Does it ever cross your mind what the origins of that car are? Yes, if it's a Toyota Camry, we know it was made from the Toyota brand. Dig deeper though. Who designed that particular model? Well, of course, the answer is the lead engineer. I encourage you to dive even deeper. Why did he or she design it? I know you're probably thinking, *Well, David, he most likely gets paid thousands of dollars to design it. I mean, come on, it's his job.* Again, go deeper than that broad explanation. Whoever that engineer was, regardless of a title or a position in any company, the car or motorcycle you just bought stemmed from an idea. That same idea gave birth to a gift. It was an idea that took thousands of hours to create, and with consistency, it involved into a gift that took hours to perfect. Now that I have your

---

[1] Alicia F. Chavez and Ronni Sanlo. *Identity and Leadership: Informing Our Lives, Informing Our Practice* (Washington: NASPA, 2003), 9

full and undivided attention, the preceding paragraphs were not meant to boost the popularity of engineers from Toyota; they formed a strategy. It's a strategy to lead you to think about the bigger picture of identity and how it relates to leadership. From the time we are born, we go through a set of experiences that form, shape, and mold us to who we are today. Experiences include a variety of factors, whether positive or negative.

Inwardness

I had the privilege of growing up in a two-parent home until I was fourteen years old. After my parents' divorce, my positive experience became a negative experience, and as result of that negative experience, my views on marriage were misconstrued. After years of struggling to find myself and figuring out who I was called to be in life, I thought I had finally realized my identity. In my senior year of high school, I was sleeping with numerous women, had college scholarships rolling in from Division I schools, and was as popular as Jay Z in a small town called Champaign, Illinois. *Wrong!* You see, I had a distorted view of reality. What seemed like a positive experience was indeed a negative experience that shaped my identity. How did I get there? Just like the engineer, it started with an idea—an idea that I wanted to come to fruition. Inadvertently, after hours of practicing how to lie to women to sleep with them, making friends, and nearly selling my soul for popularity, it all led me to a fallacy. Again, what does identity mean to you? You will have to live with the identity you create and face the positive or negative consequences of your choices. When you haughtily display your identity, it's in direct conflict of what you are portraying. My true identity was a senior in high school on the borderline of flunking out. I had a reputation as a man equal to four days of garbage, and I had two or three scholarships that barely cracked Division II and Division III schools. Remember that your identity is the culture you set within. Oops! There is that word again: *identity*. Well, since I have probed your mind to think deeper about what identity is, where do you find yours? We are aware that experiences shape our identity. When it comes to identity in the form of leadership, positive and negative experiences can mold you into a phenomenal leader. For example, I got married at the age of twenty-one years old. Numerous people thought I was ludicrous, others thought it was the beginning of a catastrophic end, but only a few saw me as an up-and-coming leader. This book is in no way, shape, or form about my accolades but about my personal experiences regarding how I identified myself. The ultimate decision that topples over all the decisions I ever made was to accept Jesus Christ as my Lord and Savior and to walk with him on a daily basis. That was my true identity, years later. In fact, throughout this book, I will elaborate on how my identity changed. You're probably wondering, *Okay, how do I recreate my identity then?*

In this book, we will talk about the four phases of what identity is and other factors that create a dynamic leader. These four stages will also give insight on recreating your identity as you see fit and what to watch out for throughout each strategy. Honestly, speaking from experience, finding your identity in something supernatural defies the laws of logic but reaps benefits that hold profit no one can purchase. Remember, your identity molds you into the leader you want to be and will become in the future. Leadership is not hindered within four church walls or in corporate America. Lastly, leadership can be as minor as setting an example to your neighbors. Identity births leadership, either positively or negatively.

So, let's recap. We exposed the core of identity and how your identity can be found in a variety of things, including money, popularity, Christ, accomplishments, or even your education. However, identity can either reap positive or negative consequences. In the next chapter, we will look at the first phase of identity.

2

Inception

Never be bullied into silence. Never allow yourself to be made a victim. Accept no one's definition of your life but define yourself.

—Harvey Fierstein

■ ■ ■

INCEPTION IS THE establishment or starting point of an institution or activity.[2] Inception is a word I use when describing dreamers. Every single person is a dreamer, whether you are three years old or sixty-three years old. Never stop dreaming, because dreamers are at the beginning stages of achieving a new identity and the creation of a standout leader.

Dream. I repeat it: dream. It's essential to believe that you are the one. You are the chosen one for a particular assignment, an inventor of a product, the CEO of a company, and even the friend a person is praying for.

Have you stopped dreaming? The real question is, why are you limiting yourself in your dreams? Remember, any

---

[2] "Inception," *Dictionary.com*, accessed January 15, 2018, http://www.dictionary.com/browse/inception.

dream created in the mind is endless. There is no cap, and the moment you cap your dreams due to external sources and/or gifts, you have immediately quit. Do you quit because of fear of failure? You're scared because it won't work out. Or maybe you are afraid that when you get to that certain place of your dream, it will end up becoming a reality and you won't be able to handle it. Again, you have quit even before you have started. The starting point of inception is the starting point. It's where you say to yourself, "I'm going back to school," "I'm going to launch this church with my team," or "I am going to lose weight and live a healthier lifestyle." Choose your starting point!

Separation

In 2013, my older brother, Dorrell Briscoe, challenged me to take a leap of faith and move from Oskaloosa, Iowa, to Jacksonville, Florida, to start a new life. Moving to Florida sparked an idea, a dream: *Wow! If I move to Florida, one day I will be rich, retire at the age of thirty, and sip margaritas on a beach. Wrong!* I was nineteen with a futile mind, and I didn't know my butt from a bagel. Little did my brother know, I was contemplating on transferring to Western Illinois University and going back to living in Illinois with a young woman I was dating at the time. In the back of mind, I knew a long-distance relationship was going to be difficult and I had doubts if it was going to work or not. After several months of contemplating, I moved down to Jacksonville, Florida, late August in 2013. You're probably thinking what happened with that young woman you were dating? Well, our relationship was on the rocks. Immediately after moving down to Florida, I dedicated my life to Christ and started walking in a new lifestyle. We both were living two different lifestyles, and I could sense we were drifting from one another. One night, after several attempts of talking to her about my new lifestyle and my beliefs in God, she quietly said, "Are you trying to be a preacher?" A preacher? Well, that was not on my list of dreams, but it sparked another idea. Several weeks later, I broke it off. In order to be a successful leader and to re-create your identity, you will have to cut some people out of your life. Yeah, it sounds harsh, and it could be a loved one, a friend, or even a family member, but your dreams don't always include people you are walking with currently. When you embark on inception, you begin to start separating yourself from other people. There lies a particular perspective, a certain uniqueness even a lifestyle that others are not accustomed to. Define your value, not in the presence of others, but in the character you construct.

Reality Check

Inception can be lonely in the beginning. You have to accept the reality that everybody won't see your dreams the way you do. Everybody will not join you on the mission you have set forth, and not everyone stays when you accomplish the dreams you lay into place. Does that mean you won't have any friends? Inception is not just a strategy and stage when you begin a new journey in life, but it's also the stage where you align yourselves with people and attract others who want to achieve the same goal. My mentor always said, "Show me your friends, David, and I will show you where you are going in life." Turn in your victim card, because you don't have to be a product of your environment. At the end of the day, it's a choice in whatever you do, so choose to surround yourselves around people who are on the same mission and mindset as to where you want to go. I broke off my relationship with that young woman because I knew where I wanted to go in life and our trajectories on what true joy and true life meant were opposite. Life threw what I like to call a "reality check." Creating an identity will have numerous reality checks, no matter what phase you are in, but especially in inception. Dreams, choices and surrounding yourself with positivity will ignite and create an identity worthwhile and increase your level of leadership in any setting, especially in the presence of a team.

I'm All In

Have you ever watched the *World Series of Poker*? When I was a kid, I used to get an adrenaline rush when a player on that show would say, "I'm all in." I would stand at the edge of my seat in expectation to see if that person was going to double up on their money or fall at the mercy of the unexpected royal flush. My favorite player was Daniel Negreanu. One year, I remember Daniel Negreanu had one of the worst hands I have seen in poker history, and he called "all in" on a late summer night. I was screaming at the TV, "WHAT ARE

YOU DOING? YOU ARE A LUNATIC!" After biting all 10 of my fingernails and pacing back in forth in my room, Daniel pulled off the impossible and won the tournament. I couldn't believe it, and I was the lunatic who was shouting because I doubted him. If you want to be defined as a fearless leader, the first step is investing in yourself. Daniel Negreanu invested in himself. Even if Daniel would have lost that tournament, in all reality, he was still going to go down as one of the greatest, if not the greatest, poker player of all time. Are you investing in yourself? What have you done this year to make those dreams come to fruition? How do you expect to see progress if you have not invested in yourself? Spend an hour with yourself alone, finish one book every month, go as far as attending a conference about learning how to become a CEO, or maybe a conference on leadership alone. Invest in yourself! Until you say, "I'm all in," you will never unlock what God called you to be on this earth.

So, let's recap: We know inception is the establishment or starting point of an institution or activity. Inception is someone who is unconsciously incompetent. Unconsciously incompetent in simple terms is someone who is embarking on a journey. You have dreamt of something superb, and now you are putting it into reality by starting a new business, going on a mission trip, or even implementing a workout regime into your daily routine. You have now cut out people in your life who don't benefit you or the dream you want to see fully realized in the future. Lastly, you have invested in yourself, whatever that may be, whether that's attending conferences, spending some money on workout clothes and running shoes or even putting a down-payment on a building to kick-off your new business. But what happens when you hit a brick wall, two or three weeks/months down the line, when you realize an over-night success story is easier said than done? We will talk about that in the next chapter, called "Deception."

3

Deception

One of the greatest tragedies in life is to lose your own sense of self and accept the version of you that is expected by everyone else.

—K.L. Toth

■ ■ ■

ASK YOURSELF, WHAT is deception? Have you gathered your thoughts? What did you come up with? I'll tell you what my thoughts are. Deception is a strategy and or method to weed out the quitters. Think of deception as this: If you asked me to break change for you, let's say $100 dollars, and I only handed you back $80 dollars, what would be your immediate response? A karate chop to the face would be extreme, but any reasonable person would react in a manner of disagreement by saying, "You just short-changed me. I need my $20, please." Identity is a safeguard, so when you embark on a new commitment or game plan for your life, your identity will say, "Hmm, no I need my $20 back." Still puzzled? Okay, let's try another example. In the summer of 2016, I took a position as a youth pastor at The City Church in Jacksonville, Florida. Funny story, I ran into Blake Bennett (senior pastor) at Forever 21 in the men's section, and God told him right there, "That is your youth pastor." It's funny because God forgot to mention that his future youth pastor loved skinny jeans. Moral of the story, after my first year of shepherding people, I started feeling the drainage of ministry. Some Christians would call this "burnout." The weight and gravity of sacrificing my life for other people started taking a toll on me. For years, I watched other pastors walk away from ministries because of the burden of leading churches and ministries. I had an ultimatum: Do I walk away for a season or two, or do I keep on fighting? The greatest fight a human will endure is the person they are and the person they are becoming. What I was becoming was the driving force of pressing forward another year. No, I could not have thrown in the white towel! Have you thrown in the white towel? No, I don't mean figuratively quit but literally where people throw in the white towel into the boxing ring. Why is that? Why can't you finish what you started? It's about to get a little personal so brace yourselves ... it's because you did not count the cost. Jesus said it perfectly in Luke 14:28-30:[28] "Suppose one of you wants to build a tower. Won't you first sit down and estimate the cost to see if you have enough money to complete it? [29] For if you lay the foundation and are not able to finish it, everyone who sees it will ridicule you,[30] saying, 'This person began to build and wasn't able to finish.'" No, we are not going to have a philosophical debate on what Jesus said or didn't say, we are talking about how you are now "consciously incompetent."

Jump

Consciously incompetent sounds a little harsh, but it should be if you want to create a new identity. You have now experienced first-hand that your new journey is tenacious. Starting this business requires you to sacrifice sleep, to spend hours documenting and reading, or even to start a workout regime; an extra 5-10 hours of working out is vigorous. You have envisioned being a CEO and having a body like Jacob from *Twilight*, but the reality is that your "old" identity is now starting to creep in. Uh oh? This is where you start to talk yourself out of it. A prime example is when I became a pastor. This was my problem, I wanted the title and not the workload. I wanted the praise and not the sacrifice. Deception is the stage where you are most vulnerable to fall back into your habitual way because venturing out to the unknown is unsafe. Venturing out into the unknown is unsafe, and your ego doesn't like it. Why? Because it's a part of your identity. Meaning if you are trying to change your identity; therefore, it would cause the death of your ego. That's what you want! The death of your ego represents a war won based on your identity. Steve Harvey said it perfectly that in life, sometimes you just have to jump, because "some of the most successful people jumped at one point in time in their life." Yes, it might sound easy, but in all reality, this stage breaks the gap between a follower and a leader. This moment defines where you will end up in 5, 10, maybe even 20 years down the line. We all have that one person, who was either a mentor, parent, relative, business partner or even a close friend who shared their defining moment. Every person will have that defining moment, but at the end of the day, it's a choice to walk in the fruits of a potential identity change.

Can you handle it?

I know you want the ring, the position, the relationship you have always desired, but can you handle it? That question should ring the bell of your soul. Can you truly handle it? That question is what few leaders ask themselves before embarking on a new mission. When you are in a dark place, ask yourself again, can you handle it? When you could potentially lose everything you have ever loved or cherished, ask yourself, can you handle it? If everyone might count you out and walk out of your life, ask yourself, can you handle it? Or even if you fail over and over and over again, ask yourself, can you handle it? I can personally guarantee you will go through darkness in order to receive the light. You might already be in a dark place as you are reading this, or you could be the one who has not yet experienced darkness. Always remember, that the dark place is a prerequisite for your greatness. Michael Ervin, in his Hall of Fame speech, said, "Every great man has been through something, a dark place." You will never achieve your most ample task until you walk through darkness. Can you handle it? You will suffer mentally, physically, and emotionally. You will cry, you will go through depression, you will experience anger, but will you endure? Oak trees grow stronger and taller when impacted by harsh winds. Can you handle it?

So, let's recap: Identity's sole responsibility is to keep us safe! Our identity stems back to what is familiar and what we are aware of. Anything that has been familiar, whether constant or habitual, suddenly ceases and your identity, your core root of who you are will still try to go out of its way and tell you to go back. Quitters always quit! Train yourself to step off the phase of deception. If you can truly handle it, the pressure, the atmosphere of doubt, it will lead to your prelude of a powerful ending! You see, there are two things you can do with pressure! The first is break or burst something, whether that's glass, a dish or even a pipe, but pressure is also used to make diamonds. When you win the war and not "if" you win the war, you will seep into a third stage called development.

4

Development

It is easier to live through someone else than to complete yourself. The freedom to lead and plan your own life is frightening if you have never faced it before. It is frightening when you finally realize that there is no answer to the question "who am I" except the voice inside you.

—Betty Friedan

■ ■ ■

DEVELOPMENT IS THE process of developing or being developed.[3] You have now worked your way up to a CEO, traveled the world to engage in missionary work or you have even seen impeccable first-hand results from the gym; you stand with an elite group of people. The development stage makes you "consciously competent." Consciously competent is when you become aware that what you are doing is resulting in profit, not just financially but mentally, physically and spiritually. You have embarked on the road of inception and fought the pressure of deception. Development is the diamond in the rough stage, where you

---

[3] Development," *Dictionary.com*, accessed January 16, 2018, http://www.dictionary.com/development.

literally grab a diamond by the hand and start the process of wiping the dirt off. The development stage is by no means the last step in the process but the dawn of a campaign worthy of efforts and sweat. You see, development is a healthy stage and it establishes the platform of a legitimate identity change. However, development is not a free access pass to slack off. Just because you now possess a new characteristic or gift or hold the key to conceiving a new identity, this does not mean a spirit of laziness should creep in. The moment you succumb the slothfulness mindset is the moment you slowly waste your gift and forfeit new ideas and opportunities. Forfeiting new ideas and opportunities have an atrocious reputation in the world. Why did I say that? We'll, let me ask you this: Do you know where the richest place in the world is? Dubai? Las Vegas? Hong Kong? It's none of the above; it's actually the grave. The richest place ever is the grave! Some of the greatest ideas, inventions, and gifts were wasted because those individuals were content on the stage of development.

Regrets

My senior year in high school, I had worked my way up to the ranks of a top hurdler in the state of Illinois. Coach Mike Shine, who was an Olympic silver medalist in the 1976 Olympics, trained me throughout my high school years. There was another local hurdler who would always go neck and neck with me at almost every single-track meet, and especially in conference/sectionals. Honestly, it sucks to admit it, but I only beat him a handful of times throughout our tenure in high school. Both of us were recruited, but he had a higher GPA and ACT score, which made him a hot commodity for more Division 1 and Division 2 colleges. Several years later, I met up with him and asked him what he was doing in life. After a lengthy conversation, he was doing quite well for himself, and of course, I brought up our glory days on what we loved to call the "hurdler life." I was itching to probe him on what Division 1 school he chose and his impeccable PR (personal record) times. He said, "You know, David, I have very few regrets, but my biggest one was never lacing up a pair of spikes and running in college." Baffled by his words, I immediately asked why, what happened, why did you quit? He said, "I was afraid that I was not going to be successful. I didn't think I was going to have the career I did in high school, so I never went to college, and I never signed. David, if you ever write a book or know someone who does, tell them the biggest poison in life is regret." DON'T waste your God-given gift, idea or even your life on a fallacy.

Consistency

Consistency, in my opinion, marks a true leader. Mark Zuckerberg, whom we all know as the founder and CEO of Facebook, has a brilliant mind. He is a billionaire, philanthropist, entrepreneur, and pioneer in the 21st century for new technology. The list goes on and on to accurately describe Mark Zuckerberg. Here is why Facebook is so consistent year in and year out: It's not just because Facebook is revolutionary but the engine and mind running the company is. Mark said in an interview, and I quote, "I wear the same shirt every day, five days ... Monday-Friday, five of the same kind of shirt." I sort of chuckled at this insane statement. Yes, 5 days out of the week. My immediate thought was, "Does this guy have a sense of style? I mean, come on, you're a billionaire, and you can't hire someone to update your wardrobe?" After pondering his statement, for a brief moment, I realized that Mark Zuckerberg operates in a consistent manner whenever he goes to work. Change is important, but consistency is revolutionary. You see, Mark Zuckerberg understands the true meaning of a consistent lifestyle, which bleeds into his business. Now, of course, I'm not advising you to go out and buy five Coogi shirts and wear them five days out of the week, but I recommend you permeate every activity of your life with the concept of consistency.

Aftermath of the storm

Have you ever read the story of King David and Bathsheba? For some who are not aware of the story, King David was hands-down one of the greatest leaders of Israel in the Old Testament. King David had numerous foes, and jealously ran rampant in the minds of his enemies. After a successful battle with the Philistines, King David came back home and was guarded physically at all times of the day/night, but spiritually, he was vulnerable. After watching Bathsheba bathe naked without bouncing his eyes, he committed one of the gravest sins, and that is adultery. As a consequence of his sin, he impregnated Bathsheba and murdered her husband to cover his butt. So now, King David had not only committed adultery, but he also committed murder and deceit. The aftermath of deception can lead to a plethora of complications if left unchecked and unguarded in the phase of "development." Development is also a stage of protection from seeping back into your old ways of life. What would David's life had looked like if he had guarded his heart and bounced his eyes or even walked away from the desires of his flesh? In the end, we will never know, but it's important to guard your heart in the heat of every moment. Hence, King David learned from his mistakes and still was beloved by his people. We can learn a lot from his story and how relevant the phases of identity are to his story. Be careful of the aftermath of the storm because every phase has a new set of challenges, even when your identity is nearing its completion.

So, let's recap: We talked about regrets in this chapter and not wasting your God-given gift, idea or even your life on a fallacy. Always remember, and keep in the back of your mind, the richest place in the world is the grave. Consistency drives the level of leadership in any person and implements a unique identity very few people achieve. Change is important, but consistency is revolutionary. Lastly, always check your heart and character after a storm. The aftermath of deception can lead to a plethora of complications if left unchecked and unguarded in the phase of "development." After three long and grueling phases, you reach the last phase in re-creating or forming your identity: metamorphosis.

5

Metamorphosis

Silent solitude makes true speech possible and personal. If I am not in touch with my own belovedness, then I cannot touch the sacredness of others. If I am estranged from myself, I am likewise a stranger to others.

—Brenna Manning

■ ■ ■

IF YOU'RE A biology major or a graduate in that field, you know exactly where I'm going with the idea of metamorphosis. This idea is applicable in science, but it also complements the next stage in an identity change. Metamorphosis is a striking alteration in appearance, character, or circumstance.[4] However, metamorphosis can be natural or supernatural. Metamorphosis is the stage where you cross the border that very few people experience let alone live out. Congratulations, you have a fresh identity! Wait? You didn't think you were done yet, did you? Oh no, there is more. You have a few more chapters to go, buddy. Just because you have created an identity does not mean you've

---

[4] "Metamorphosis," *Merriam-Webster,* accessed January 11, 2018, https://www.merriam-webster.com/dictionary/metamorphosis.

made it. For years, my identity was built on my older brother, Dorrell. Yes, we had similar accomplishments, but someone once bluntly said to me, "You are only what you are because of your brother." Dang, was it true? Had I built the premises of my life from my older brother? Honestly, for years, I tried to be a person that I was not. Yeah, pride got in the way and blinded me from seeing the bigger picture, but I realized that I was walking in a false identity.

You see, once you build an identity, you will fall under what I like to call someone who is "unconsciously competent." Have you ever seen an athlete implement the same fundamentals in a football or basketball game that they operated in practice? Are you still a little confused on what unconsciously competent is? How many of you watched Super Bowl 51? Tom Brady, who in my opinion is the GOAT (Greatest Of All Time), won that game based off not just talent but by being "unconsciously competent." If you want to debate on who is the GOAT, now is not the appropriate time; that is what Facebook is for. Unconsciously competent is someone who spends tens of thousands of hours perfecting their identity regardless of how good or bad their identity is. Tom Brady once said in an interview that even when he is on vacation, he still watches film and studies his playbook. Unconsciously competence is the critical driving force to maintaining a stable identity.

Re-evaluation

So, you think you're a leader, huh? *Wrong!* You still have a lot more work. Re-evaluation marks a leader and reminds him/her of what needs to be changed. Re-evaluation is another crucial step in maintaining the status quo. Being unconsciously competent is embedded in one's nature unless re-evaluation drives it out. Re-evaluation is the key to unlocking the door within one's soul, and it holds the potential to bring awareness to any and all identity change. Every impactful leader will re-evaluate himself. Most leaders in today's society think they fall under a sort of deity identity or they place themselves in an imaginary kingdom they rule. A profound leader observes not only his heart but the way he leads his care of span. Think of a re-evaluation as this. Let's swap the roles, and say I work for you at a small business that sells coffee. You are the supervisor on duty, and I work as the cashier. Every Wednesday, you will have all the staff meet to discuss how to keep customers engaged with conversations with their friends and how to improve customer services. Let's say I come up with a useful idea that would implement a way to improve customer service and potentially keep customers an extra thirty minutes in the coffee shop. As far-fetched as it may be, the moment I finish my sentence, you blurt out, "Nope, that's not going to work." Number 1, you are lucky I am saved and sanctified because you would have received a few words that would not be pleasant. Number 2, you don't know how to accept the truth and number 3, you just failed and are inadequate leader who cannot take heed to someone else's ideas. Being a leader means having the ability to identify other people's strengths and bring them together to make something bigger than themselves. Think about it, what's the first thing you say when someone offers you a gift? The immediate response is, "thank you," or "oh my gosh … I love you, thanks." As a leader, any new idea or method your team comes up with, embrace it, say thank you for their input and consider putting it into practice. The keyword is "consider," which means you don't always say yes but acknowledging the idea should deserve praise, and it in return, drives out the fear of that idea being shot down. Honestly, the same method should be used if you were to ask a person who is under your leadership "How am I leading?" Try it out. Ask someone who is under your care of leadership and say, "How I am leading? What are some things that I can improve on?" You may not always get an honest answer because some people care more about their job than your well-being or leadership goals. However, you may get a couple of truthful nuggets here and there, and those are worth more than any dollar earned, building built or customer attained because you have earned an honest suggestion that will carry the trajectory on your leadership to a favorable ending if you are mindful of that suggestion.

Sustainability

Have you earned your spot? With the new identity you have created, the new and improved you, the fresh style of leadership you have created in your ministry, small-business or even non-profit, have you earned your spot? Let's say you have, but how do you sustain your level of leadership or focus? God has created and implemented everything on this earth not just for a purpose but a method on how it is going to be sustained. Prime example is this: Whenever you get hungry, what is the first thing that pops into your head? Tacos? When you get hungry, and if you're in the mood for tacos, where do you go? My favorite restaurant is a hole-in-the-wall that is roughly 20 minutes from my house, and they sell some infamous Mexican food. That small-business has a system in place that reciprocates itself that keeps me coming back time and time again. That hole-in-the-wall restaurant has a system that has sustainability; they have created a system to limit overhead costs and to concentrate more on the product and customer service that allows them to deliver inevitable results every single day. As a result, they keep customers like myself coming back on a weekly basis. In leadership, you need to create a system that reciprocates to the point where people admire and love your style of leadership, and it inspires them to walk in the same fruits of your labor. If you don't have a system in a variety of areas in your life, how do you expect to lead people? How can you sustain your level of leadership if you don't have a system? Take a step back, and ask yourself, am I feeding what is feeding me? Seriously, are you sustaining or are you surviving? You will never make it if you are just trying to survive, but if you organize and feed the system that is feeding you, you will sustain every single season of your life.

So, let's recap: We discussed how to operate in a unconsciously competent mindset, where you don't have to think about it; you just get it done. Those people who whenever they are traveling for leisure know that 6 am workouts are mandatory are no exceptions. Also, we talked about how being a leader is having the ability to identify other people's strengths and bring them together to make something bigger than themselves. Re-evaluating your leadership periodically allows clearance for people who are under you to suggest gold nuggets that could potentially strengthen your leadership. Lastly, you must have a system in place. Systematic people lead in a systematic manner. Always remember to depart from inception, conquer deception, fasten to development and ingrain metamorphosis. Identity is the final stage but never the final stage.

6

Unity

"One family, many faces. One family, many races. One truth, many paths. One heart, many complexions. One light, many reflections. One world, many imperfections. ONE. We are all one, but many."

—Suzy Kassem

■ ■ ■

CARL LENTZ, ONE of the pastors on staff at Hillsong Church in New York, wrote a book called *Own the Moment* and titled one of his chapters "If You Are Racist and You Know It, Clap Your Hands." This chapter might bring some sensitivity to some people but after careful planning and prayer, I do believe it will change the perspective on what unity looks like in a leader. Where do I start? Well, just like Carl Lentz said, "If you are a racist, clap your hands." What is a racist, though? A racist is a person who shows or feels discrimination or prejudice against people of other races, or who believes that a particular race is superior to another. Let's focus on superiority first. If in any way shape or form you feel you are superior to your peers and the people who lead, you are a racist. Not only are you a racist, but that mindset automatically disqualifies you from a dynamic leader. I'm baffled that we as a nation do not understand the concept of superiority and the context by which it's used. Superiority in the form of racism is not a white man/woman looking down on a minority as less efficient or intelligent, which is partially correct. Prime example, if you are a minority, whether black, Hispanic and or Asian, and you think or speak in a negative fashion upon another race because you feel as if your race is more dominant in that profession or just in general ... news flash: you are a racist. This past year, I heard an African American man, probably in his late 30s, honk at a young Asian woman driving, and he zipped past her and flicked her off. When I pulled up next to him at the light, we both had our windows down and he was still using profanity describing how Asians can't drive. Again, that person is a racist. How can you lead others when you cannot even lead yourself in your way of thinking? Jesus was a role model in racial reconciliation. In John Chapter 4 verse 7-45, Jesus began speaking with a woman who was a Samaritan. Quick little history lesson: Back in those days, when Jesus walked the earth, Jews had absolutely no dealings with Samaritans. In fact, later in that chapter, John (Jesus' disciple) wrote how he marveled that Jesus was talking to a Samaritan woman and how he thought, "Why is Jesus talking to a woman like her?" Futile in their thinking, Jesus understood how to bridge the culture gap. Jews were superior, and the Samaritan people were outcasts. You may be reading this and have no interest in Christianity, but you have to acknowledge Jesus' intentions to heal the Samaritan woman's broken life and to bridge the spiritual and social aspect of Jews and Samaritans. In verse 16-26, Jesus mends and heals her heart spiritually but simultaneously, he is speaking with her as a normal human being, which in turns heals her heart socially in dealings with Jews. How you interact and respond to others who are placed in your life will define your leadership. Jesus recognized the culture gap and broke its subliminal barriers, and that is why is he counted as one of the greatest teachers of all time. Dynamic leaders find a way to include all races and demographics.

Colin Kaepernick

What was your immediate reaction when you read that name? Some of you became instantly uncomfortable. Others nodded their head in an agreement because you would count Colin as a leader, and many are contemplating putting this book down because you are angry about what he represents. If you are in the category of putting this book down or instantly feeling uncomfortable, we have much to discuss. However, if you do end up putting this book down halfway through this next section or even afterwards because of your disagreement with my words, you prove the previous paragraph accurately and in turn exclude yourself and others from seeing the finished product of your leadership. First things first, let's talk about if you felt uncomfortable. Some may claim he is sort of divisive and unappealing by his moral actions. Let's get to the root and ask, what about his moral actions makes you uncomfortable? Hmmm, let me take a wild guess ... is it because it's about race? Let's be honest, we all don't like to talk about racism, because its uncomfortable. Someone might get offended or you might not know much about it. Your uncomfortableness can lead to the misery of your peers by the lack of your expression and unwillingness to speak up. As a pastor, I believe God can move past natural laws, so we can operate under spiritual laws. I'm also a firm believer that he can change the heart of any man or woman who is walking this planet. However, that should not be a scapegoat to avoid the duty of speaking up about racism. Leaders speak up when necessary and not only when it is convenient.

Are you almost at the point of dropping this book? No, I'm not mocking you. I'm challenging you to change your perspective on leadership in the context of unity. Right about now, you are thinking to yourself, why the heck is Pastor David defending the cause and actions of Colin Kaepernick? Pause … Why are you so angry? Just recently, I was working for a company here in Jacksonville, Florida, that required three weeks of intensive training. On the very first day, we had to show our two forms of ID to an older lady who was the head of Human Resources. As we were waiting for our names to be called, I could not help to see the sorrowful and grievant faces of my peers gazing at the TV. "Mass shooting in Las Vegas." I was puzzled and troubled in my spirit to hear the number of men and women who had lost their lives and who were severely injured by a senseless shooting. To be honest, I was hurt because I knew that families were affected tremendously, and that mourning process began a hundred-fold. Later on, in that day, we were required to engage in an interactive game with whoever was sitting next to us. A young woman and I conversed briefly. I have no clue how we got on the conversation, but she disclosed to me how she just recently moved to Jacksonville from Las Vegas and how she had friends who were victims of the shootings. My first reaction was shock. I had so many questions running throughout my mind but for some reason, I could not put them into words. Instead of trying to sort out of my thoughts into words, I just sat back and listened. This young woman poured out her heart to someone she didn't even know and I could feel her anguish. It was no more than twelve hours from this reckless shooting and it was like I could feel the agony of that unbearable situation. Colin Kaepernick does not want you to just listen to the words that come out of his mouth or the anguish he feels when he sees racial injustice on the news; Colin wants you to hear the words and frantic cries of the parents who have lost their children and relatives to racism. Stop pointing your finger at Kaepernick and listen carefully to those cries whose families do not catch media attention. Only then will you truly understand unity. Numerous people ask me how Colin Kaepernick can be counted as a leader, especially a leader of unity, when he disrespects the American flag. It's interesting how we immediately jump to how Kaepernick disrespected the flag, but we have yet to elaborate on the issue in which why he kneeled. As a leader, Kaepernick understood that in order to create unity, we must first address the issue at hand. My older brother always warned me that "in leadership, people will hate your guts." In any form of leadership you operate in, there will be naysayers, people who disagree with your actions, but it's up to you to keep striving to bring harmony, influence and unity to your sphere.

    I have not forgotten about the ones who nodded their head in agreement with Colin Kaepernick. You still have just as much to learn about unity. Just because you neglect the power of division does not mean you have all the answers to embrace and birth unity. The issue is never the issue; the issue is the tool that society will use to create division. Unity has strength in numbers, which in packs can overcome any obstacle placed in its path. Have you ever looked outside at the stars when it's super dark outside? You never knew the stars were there until it was dark enough; hence, you truly never know a person until you realize the darkness one person has been through and rally that individual, regardless of color. Overall, unity is not a gift that is stemmed from leadership; it's acquired through persistence and constant effort to include all people who bring their own uniqueness to the table.

So, let's recap: We talked in detail about what counts as a racist. It is someone who is silent to racism, which is the antonym of unity. How you interact and respond to others who are placed in your life will define your leadership. We also discussed what moral consequences leaders will face when trying to implement unity in any setting. Lastly, we brought awareness and shed light on racism, which in turn will dampen a leader's full potential. I hope and pray that this chapter challenged you to step out in boldness and bring you out of your comfort zone.

7

Opportunity

When things do not go your way, remember that every challenge — every adversity — contains within it the seeds of opportunity and growth.

—Roy T. Bennett

■ ■ ■

IF YOU HAD one shot or one opportunity to seize everything you ever wanted, in one moment, would you capture it or just let it slip? Yes, I just quoted Eminem; get over it. In all reality, as a leader, would you seize the opportunity or would you let it slip right through your fingers? That's a question that all leadership books should ask, but very few would challenge you to question what your life looks before that moment. We don't all have equal opportunity, privileges are distributed contingent upon your social status or how many zeroes you have in your bank account but we ALL have the opportunity to improve who we currently are to prepare us for that special moment. Moments are critical for the direction of our lives, but what makes moments special? Is it the opportunity to seize political or cultural power over your peers? Or is that the tingling feeling you get when you are about to prove all the people wrong who doubted you? Either way, you have the opportunity to create that special moment and the will to execute it. But how are those moments of opportunity distributed? Could it be luck or being at the right place at the right time? Was it an overnight success or was it a consistent dedication to align that opportunity with reality? I'm amazed at my generation, the "millennials." We want an opportunity to succeed, to be a difference-maker in society, yet we lack the basic fundamentals to create those opportunities and moments. As millennials, we want to rub the magic genie, be given an opportunity that we expect to fall in our laps and then try to seize the moment by our arrogant and pathetic measures of greatness. Yes, it's very harsh, but it is the honest truth. Baby boomer's mock millennials because we lead by social media but lack the fundamentals to operate in leadership in real life. My pops would call those type of people "pretenders." Yes, I am talking about myself as well because I once was a pretender. I was idled and unproductive, expecting a spoon in my mouth, lacking the mechanics to create an opportunity because I was futile in my thinking. I wanted to so many things in life but I refused to allow success in my life. You can't have it all at once! The first thing you have to learn about opportunities is that opportunities appear in increments. I heard someone say on campus one-time, "I want to be a millionaire, but I don't want to work." That person failed to realize that in order to become a millionaire, you first have to have a job or an investment. A job leads to a promotion. A promotion could potentially make you a partner and then the sole owner of a company. Boom! You have become a millionaire, because you got a job. Increments make the bridge between opportunity and another opportunity. The decisions you make today will determine your tomorrow and your opportunities. When I desired all those things, I never created a bridge to parallel my efforts, which limited my opportunities. Opportunities will define your life, but what's your definition of your life if you fail to even create the opportunity?

Opportunities that seem insignificant

Take your opportunities seriously! Every day, I wake up and I am amazed by what the Lord has blessed me with. Every little opportunity prepared me for what was in store for me years later in life. My wife always brings up on when she first saw me working at a local movie theater. I always brag that she was dazzled by my smile and personality. Jasmine watched me numerous times as I was serving popcorn and candy to people. Her words were, "Wow ... he has so much potential; he is beyond this job." Honestly, I look back on that job that only paid minimum wage to stand on my feet for almost 8 hours a day, and I rejoice because it was a stepping stone. Two things I learned from that job was how to serve and honor people who disrespect you. Trust me, when you are five minutes late for the Harry Potter movie, situations can get ugly very quickly. That job was insignificant, but I valued it even though it paid minimum wage. Life lessons can be poured out during an insignificant opportunity in your everyday life. Day in and day out, I learned how to serve people in a manner of humility and honor. Every now and then I would have someone disrespect me. Heck I even had "racial slurs" whispered under their breath as I was buttering their popcorn. However, I never let that change my attitude or the way I honored people. Whatever position you are in life right now, cherish that opportunity, even if its minor. Always remember that someone is watching and will see your potential, just like my wife did for me. Having someone who believes in you while you are in a season of a position that may seem insignificant can be rewarding in the end.

Decisions, decisions ... decisions

Are your decisions a dead-end or a new beginning? Let's take a step back: Have you ever seen snow? People who live in the Midwest would probably read this and nod their head with grievance. Well, even if you have not, every person has at least seen a snow angel. As a kid, I enjoyed making snow angels, running out in fresh snow and sweeping my arms and legs back and forth. There was a kid who would always ruin my snow angels and draw a long line through it. Yeah, he stopped that quickly when he was sucker-punched in the face. Don't sucker-punch someone in the face for ruining your snow angels; that's not the moral of the story of playing Rocky Balboa in the snow. The real moral of the story is the decision. Failure is a decision, mediocracy is a decision and seizing the moment is a decision. Is it fair to say that anything you have desired in your life was or is so close to becoming a reality in your life that you can literally taste it? Inspiring leaders know how to step into uncertainty and bring the certainty into the situation. Great leaders know how to make the decision when it truly counts. A leader envisions what he/she wants, changes the tempo and has already seized the moment before the moment or opportunity is even raised. Why? Because impactful leaders already know what the moment feels like; it's been implanted in their minds and hearts before the opportunity presents itself. In order to seize the moment and opportunity, envision the feeling first and feed your mind with the outcome you already dreamt of.

So, let's recap: We elaborated on what it looks like to seize the opportunity. We don't all have equal opportunity; privileges are distributed contingent upon your social status or how many zeroes you have in your bank account, but we ALL have the opportunity to improve who we currently are to prepare us for that special moment. We also discussed being thankful and content in the position or season of life you are in. Opportunities that seem insignificant can play a key role in another opportunity in life. Cherish that opportunity, even its minor. Lastly, we talked about how great leaders know how to step into uncertainty and bring the certainty into the situation. You have to take advantage of an opportunity of a lifetime and the lifetime of the opportunity!

8

Servitude

Everybody can be great ... because everybody can serve. You don't have to have a college degree to serve. You don't have to make your subject and verb to agree. You only need a heart full of grace. A soul generated by love.

—Dr. Martin Luther King Jr.

■ ■ ■

WHAT WILL THE end of your life look like? I know you're probably thinking, what kind of question is that? Seriously though, when you are at the end of your life, what will it look like and what will your thoughts be? My wife and I went to visit my grandmother when she was very sick. We almost thought we lost her. On our flight from Florida to Illinois, all I could think about was her and if I was going to get a chance to speak with her before she passed away. As we arrived in Illinois, we immediately left the airport and drove to her house. My grandma was shocked and deeply joyful that we flew to see her. Our conversation lasted for hours. My grandma was telling her whole life story, stories that I had never even heard of. I was intrigued because I realized that my grandma accomplished a lot in her lifetime. However, towards the end of our conversation, she said, "God is the author and finisher of our faith." Tears started rolling down my cheek because here was a woman who was near the end of her life, talking about how when she first gave her heart to Christ in her 20s and now in her 80s, she was still talking about the same person who radically changed her life. Astonished by her faith, that was not the only thing that sparked my attention. I noticed that she would always talk about how different people were impacted by not only her leadership but her service to others. One thing I will never forget is when she said, "David, no matter what position you are given in life, always make sure you serve others … no matter what it looks like."

Of course, a well-mannered grandson would say, "Of course Grandma, I will." You see at the end of your life, whether you are laying on your death bed or taking your last breath, you are not going to be worrying about how much money you had, how much power or prestige you had. I believe the only thing that will matter is what impact you had on other people's lives. How are people impacted by the way you serve them? What changed or who changed because of the initiative you took to say I will sacrifice and serve others even if I get nothing back in return? I don't know about you but as a leader, when I pass away and when a family member or my wife speaks on my eulogy, I want people to know how David Briscoe lived, how he loved others and how he sacrificed and laid down his life to serve others. Servitude is an act of obedience and the humility that changes the lives of even the lowest people. Servitude should give you a sense of hope that you don't get to walk this planet in vain. My grandma knew that because she was on this earth, she had a responsibility to change not only her heart but the hearts of others through her serving. Don't leave this earth without blessing the lives of others from your service.

A servant's heart

Christian or non-Christian, there is no debate on whether Jesus was a tremendous leader or not. We know that Jesus was indeed controversial in his time, but he impacted generation after generation after his death because of his teachings. There is a lesson that should be taught in every school that leaders lack in society because of the willingness to serve. We serve out of obligation and not from the heart. Think about the countless times people drive past homeless men and women who don't even roll down their window to offer a dollar. Or better yet, the numerous non-profits and Christian ministries that feed the homeless and very few offer an hour to serve someone less fortunate than themselves. Hear me out, I'm not accusing anyone of such accusations, but can you feel the world is becoming colder and harsher? Where have we gone wrong? I believe we forgot that important teaching that Jesus portrayed 2,000 years ago and that is to not only serve but having the "willingness" to serve. Think about a man who very much gave up his royal authority to come down to earth and not only preach a message of hope but of forgiveness. In doing so, he brought along twelve unique individuals to walk alongside him in his journey, which is another sermon in itself and washed his disciple's feet. He taught his disciples and the coming generations an important lesson: It does not matter where you rank in society, what social class or political party you are affiliated with; simply serve others. Pause and meditate on that for a second. This was a man who got on his knees and lowered himself, so others would see his heart for humanity. Maybe you need to serve others more in your life. If you are not a fan of Jesus, take a look of some of the most profound humanitarian's in the world. They serve not be noticed or to receive Facebook/Instagram likes; they serve because it's embedded within their soul to see the world change one person at a time.

The Indispensable currency

The service you offer to people whether financially, physically, or even emotionally is the most valuable currency on this planet. No one can take away a changed heart, a changed mind or even a changed soul. A million dollars can be very useful in anyone's life, but if you can change a life by giving your free-time to see a life change, pass on the million dollars. Yeah, I get it, it's a lot of money, but the mark of servitude you leave on a generation may never fade.

So, let's recap: We talked in depth on how a leader serves. At the end of your life, you will evaluate your success and accomplishments, but ultimately, what will really matter is the impact you left on this world by your willingness to serve. If you want to become a dynamic leader, serve in a dynamic way. Servitude is the ultimate act of humility. Lastly, the most indispensable currency on this planet is to serve people in a financial, physical or even mental manner. What legacy and leadership will you leave?

9

Failure

You may encounter many defeats, but you must not be defeated. In fact, it may be necessary to encounter the defeats, so you can know who you are, what you can rise from, how you can still come out of it.

—Maya Angelou

■ ■ ■

WHEW! THIS IS a chapter I know all too well. This chapter in my opinion is the most important chapter of them all. In fact, I want to imagine that I am sitting on your couch and we are having a cup of coffee, sharing my life story with you, as if I had subliminally not already done that. To be honest, we really don't need to describe failure. It's straight-forward and simplistic. In leadership, you will experience this countless times, and I want to encourage you on what steps to take on how to pick yourself. A righteous man will fall 77 times, but he will get back up each and every time. Alright, enough of the small talk, let's get to the nitty-gritty. In July of 2016, my wife and I were going 6 months strong into marriage. A young woman from my past reached out to me on Facebook and asked for a DNA test for her son. Looking at this little cute munchkin, I realized that he looked just like me. Several weeks later, the DNA results came back positive that he was my son. My first reaction was pure joy, a little boy named Izzak. Unfortunately, not everyone had the same views as me and in fact, instead of receiving joy and celebration, I experienced hate and mockery. Immediately, I received resentment, mockery and disgust from everyone I could think of. People in the church, family members, friends and others who barely even knew me. To be honest, I was baffled and hurt that even the closest people to me would crack jokes and resent the fact that I have a son, out of all things. I wrestled with God for months and didn't want to speak to anybody. In fact, I was angry that God wanted me to look the same people in the eyes who had so much to say and continually pray and love them. There were times when I could hear the Lord say to me, "Pray for those who persecute you, even the ones who are the closest to you," and I refused. I shook my fist at God and said, "Why? I don't owe them anything." Failure in the eyes of others consumed me. I was bitter, depressed and angry. My sweet wife one day looked at me and said, "David, you are going to be a wonderful father, so silence the voices of others." Her sweet words instantly brought healing; everything I needed to hear in one sentence brought my soul from anguish to peace. The failure was not that I had a son before marriage; the failure was that I fed into lies and into the hate of others. I failed because their opinions outweighed what God had already spoken to me. I failed my wife and failed God because I allowed an individual to value my worth as a father and pastor. I failed because I accepted the falsehood that leaders require perfection in all areas of life in order to impact people. Hear my words, failure is inevitable as a leader but how you handle failure will define your story. You see, I had every right to act in the manner that I operated in and I could have stayed bitter and resentful, but where would that have gotten me? In leadership, you will fail countless times and people will look at you as if you were the next OJ Simpson case but embrace the resentment and keep on loving people who don't love you. Failure will mark your leadership and build you until something greater than what you see in the mirror today. Failure is simply a plateau and vision of the future you.

The Failure of Others

What happens if people fail you? It hurts when you expected something from someone close to you, whether it was a family member, a friend or even co-worker that you trusted. When they not only failed but failed you multiple times, how do you react? This is an important question, especially due to the fact that in leadership, no one is perfect, and sooner or later, you will have a person who drops the ball. Take for instance Jesus and Judas. Jesus who handpicked each and every disciple to walk with him on a three journey with him. City after city, Jesus modeled what it looked like to walk this earth with integrity and love. Does it ever spark your curiosity that Jesus knew first-hand that Judas was going to betray him before it even popped into Judas mind? Three years is a very long time, especially when you are in close proximity of someone. Countless times, Jesus looked Judas and his disciples into the eyes and showed unconditional love. The fact that a man could love a person relentlessly, time and time again, when Jesus knew he was going to betray him and yet continually pour passionate love models the leadership that we should follow. As a direct result of Judas' actions, Jesus was flogged and tortured to the brink of death and said, "Father, forgive them for they know not what they do." Judas failed Jesus and yet he still honored him. When your employees, friends, co-workers and even family members fail you, remember to honor and respect them. Profound leaders know that it's not a matter of "if" but a matter of "when" people fail that you will truly see their value and recognize their potential to overcome.

So, let's recap: This chapter was a little more intimate. We talked about how as a leader you will experience failures countless times, but failure is never the end of your story; it is merely a hurdle of a future victory. Also, we discussed what it looks like when someone fails you. Profound leaders know how to cherish an individual after a failure and motivate them to push forward. Failures can either make you a monster or a leader.

10

The Prize

We should not judge people by their peak of excellence; but by the distance they have traveled from the point where they started.

—Henry Ward Beecher

■ ■ ■

CONGRATULATIONS, YOU MADE it! The last and final chapter is "the prize." The prize is not what you do better as a leader, but it is cherishing the platform of leadership. No, I'm not saying you should become arrogant and abuse your position but take a step back one day and look at what you have built, look at the lives you have touched because of your fearless leadership. Your leadership has inspired up-and-coming leaders to slowly crack open their shell of leadership, and that was only because you made that happen. Identity, inception, deception, development, metamorphosis, unity, opportunity, servitude, sacrifice and lastly the prize all shape and mold a leader and the leaders who will be needed for tomorrow. Identity is the blueprint and the building-block for leadership. Inception is the prelude of a journey worth taking, and deception is the stumbling block for an inspirational story. The development bridges the gap between good and great leaders, while metamorphosis is the beautiful butterfly that elegantly flies after a rigorous process. Unity is the inclusion of all races and nationalities, and opportunity is that little voice in the back of your head that compels you to steer toward your dream. Servitude is lowering yourself to elevate the gifts and people around you. Sacrifice is giving up your well-being and comfort for the projection of the mission and lastly "the prize" is the reflection of your efforts and hard-work.

Death

We talked a little about death in the previous chapters, but what will the end of your life look and what legacy will you leave because of the impact you had on others. Let's go deeper. We all know that death is something that is guaranteed and unexpected. Death can happen in a fraction of a second or years to the end result. Regardless, death is never a joyous moment. It's a moment of sadness and tears. However, a leader should rejoice in death because it's the ending to not just the journey of leadership but the ending of a precious life that was lived out in full. My high-school football coach would always tell me, "David, when you die … die on E, accomplish everything in this lifetime and you will rest in the next." As a leader, don't just reflect the fruits of your labor at the brink of death but each and every day in whatever leadership capacity you operate in. I will leave you this quote that changed my life forever and inspired me to write this book. Jim Carrey once said, "Life is a mirror and life gives us not what we want; life gives us who we are. When you were born, you cried while the world rejoiced …… live your life in such a way that when you die, the world cries while you rejoice."

I'm David Dishon Briscoe! Thank you for reading!

www.ingramcontent.com/pod-product-compliance
Lightning Source LLC
Chambersburg PA
CBHW031549210526
45464CB00003B/1220